MANGROVES OF MY MIND

NAMRATA

Writing has always been with me since the time I knew what heartbreak was. Someone said that to be a writer, you should be in love or heartbroken. In the most vulnerable of my times, I later sat with a pen and a notebook, which changed to my phone notes. I would like to dedicate this book to my 18-year-old self who thought she couldn't achieve much in her life.

Contents

Preface

When I was 23 years old, back in 2015 I had to face a question from my then-boss as to what my passion was. It didn't even take me a second to answer it was publishing a book. Yes. It was not even writing, it was publishing a book. Ever since I started reading out fiction books, it was my dream to write a book, and publish it. On the days i used to wander in bookshops, I wished i could see a book on the shelf with my name on it. On the course of these years, I had written many poems which gave me solace in my heart broken moments. In this book you could see those poems. Some reflecting my love, anger and sadness.

Acknowledgements

My mother has always been a hero figure in my life. Thanks to her for standing by me to support all my dreams and decisions. I would also like to thank my partner of 7 years, for standing beside me to guide me through my toughest times. He will and always be my best friend. My in-laws without whom I couldn't even dare to dream. They have been the biggest supporters of my journey. My aunts, uncle, my brothers, and sisters stood alongside me during my toughest times. My crazy friends have always been there.

Prologue

It was the best of times

It was the worst of times

Immersed in foolishness

Drowned in compassion

Holding on tight with kindness

Pouring out on a paper

1. Hidden

Stupid you call me, for not telling him
Through thick and thin we stood
Friends for him, Devotion for me
World stood still when he was around
People said we were friends much
unfortunately to him also
we shared everything under the sun
I wanted to tell him,how much he meant to me
Years passed by,couldn't gather courage to tell
we are best friends though
"THEY MAKE A GooD PAIR" i told to my frnd
trying to hide a tear while they walked past by

2. Lost

I wish together and forever
I could dream on the days by.
You look at me, and don't see me
The best was to hold you tight.
To feel when you are there
Having your hand rest upon me.
I follow you thee, just to meet you once

Down the street I see another figure.
Eyes turned pale and I turned to run
Thinking that you stabbed me with a knife.
There was never another one for me
But you had to choose between lots.
You never knew how I feel
And I still am confused.

3. Outline

Looking through the window pane
I stare at your dwindling stature.
Still have a hope, to be back
I long for your voice and touch.

In the hazy smog, I see you
A shiver ran through my body.
Brittle face of mine, has tears down
You said me those words, finally.
Trying to hold you on tight.
But all I could see was an outline waning.

4. Unsolved

I look at myself in the mirror
I see an unsolved mystery
I am hurt inside

Hopes that fall and love which died
Blood doesn't shed out anymore,
Yet the scars shows it all

The pain still remains
The tears still fall off
I can't help it all

How is that I cry all along?
Yet all you do was to smile
Give me some light to bear.

Replay what we were once
I can't believe it's done now
Let me breath once again.

Wait baby, just wait a sec
I can't let you go away.
I can't give up what we had
I just can't forget it.

5. Torn

On my pillow I rest my head
Which is viscous with fear
Witnessing the fight with a teardrop
Rage conquers my mind
I wonder though u dream of me?

A faint cry could ease the pain
I still long for my better days.
Loneliness gives me strength
To wait for someone inside to arrive.

Be with me now and forever
As a new life beings for us.
Your touch makes my token
It l be here for long enough.

As I remain here broken
Depressed and sadness follow me all
I lay on my womb and cry
Thinking the fate of him.

6. Again

Today I love you more
Than I can say
Look at the date,
Eleven months ago.
You invited me in
To a life and a love,
That neither of us could win.
I gave you my all,
I gave you my heart
Now I'm here alone
All torn apart.
We began so happy
Without promise or fear,
Supposed to be our year
Mine and yours
I felt so lucky
So happy I was with you,
you made me laugh
Smile and cry,
But no matter what
I'll love you till I die.
In the end
You walked away,
Although I tried
I couldn't make you stay.

7. Choice

I tried so hard
To keep you here
But your choice was made,
It was done and clear.
I wish I could hold you
I wish you could see
That without you here,
I'm no longer me.
It is so hard
Harder than you know
Because now I can see
I have to let you go.
It should be us,
You and me
I wish I could say
you are mine

8. Always

I now realize
You are truly gone,
That you never loved me
That you've moved on.
I can't sleep,
Think or breathe,
All because
You decided to leave.
You were my life,
My dreams come true
My one true love,
You know that was you.
But I'll be strong and not cry,
You leave me with no choice
But to say I love you and goodbye
And a promise that I ' love u always ..

9. Remember

I met this guy

I try to remember thy

Once we Dated

He Grew up in City

But doesnt have the maturity.

When I met him again

The memories took me back,

The time I spent with him

All the good laughs and tears we shared came into my mind

But all he brought for me was pain and misery.

Soft music fills the air

I take my guitar and feather up a string,

Only to make my memories fade away.

Drowning in nothing but Fear !!

Fear of you again coming back into my life.

Coz I am now over on you..

And pls dnt make me go swirl as u did once.

10. Lie

When you say I love you
I can understand it was a lie!
I don't wanna be played
again and again by your lies
You are giving me more and more pain
and i just wanna scream loud
Just stop it right way!
The way you lie..
I cant stop from loving you
each day pass by its getting deeper and deeper

My heart wanna hate you
not to love you anymore
but its just a wish,
coz i cant do it.

11. Smile

You know that I never smiled
After that day,when we became two.
I can't smile without you
I can't live without you.
Its been a nightmare,living
My whole life,thinking of the past.
I'm finding it hard now,
As you are again near me.
I feel sad when you are crying,
I feel angry when you are hurt.
Is that because,you never knew
That I can't smile without you.
You came along just like a wind
And touched my skin as soft as it would be.
When you came along,I cried my pain
Screaming out in loud,to let people hear.
That I can't smile without you

12. Truth

Heart is the place
Where secrets are opened
An eager to wait
For the day to come

All you said,was a word
A truth by all means

There I wait
Burning away my pains
Sealed by fear
Just for the day

I waited so long for you to tell me
That all you said was a lie

Given the facts
What I know was true
I always thougt that you loved me
I always wanted you to tell me the truth

Then why was it this way
A tear ran through my cheek
When you said that truth
You never loved me , I didnt know

But when you said
There was someone
To be filled my place
I was crushed

Coz you never knew that
No one could replace
You in my heart and soul
Forever the truth is left!

13. Betrayal

When you tasted the Betrayal
They seem so true
You think you see them
But we don't
its just another illusion.

Air smell like a sordid aroma
Nothing seems right
A scream let out
Nothing feels the same
Lies are all we taste
Like a childs yelp
Everything feel wrong.

A Crusade is through
Odor of a terapidation
I can smell Betrayal here
To the ambiguity of the knife
Which is sealed in me
They can smell my fear
The perfume of yours
Have caught in their eyes

They stabbed me from the back
I couldn't move,but yearn for help

I just wanted love
I just wanted you
I never imagined to be betrayed
I had the taste of it!

14. Wall

A Glass wall being built
Around me to keep you out
My ears couldn't bear the shouting
And my heart couldn't bear the pain.

You who has no feelings
Who is hard as a rock can be
Your savge attitude
Will never give you good things
And here I am leave you with a cry.

I will not feel sorry for the things
My feelings have died for you
Just like Moon turn back to stars

Letting you know
That I am over you
Its been hard to let you go
And I ve moved on with my life

15. Bench

That bench in the park
I can never forget
As you have given me all
What I can never repay.

You have taken the charm
My eyes are wet in harm
I can always think
To the good old days.

What have you done to me?
I can never sit and gaze upon
Those wonderful days again
On that bench which is left alone.

The snow which has covered
My mind and the bench
Can never be earsed
As it has crushed my mind alas!

16. Wonder

Sitting out in a grassy field
While I watch the sun set
In this distant horizon
I always wonder
How long it will take me
To completely forget you

So yes,it hurts, it always will
And it's like going through hell trying to keep still
Trying not to get restless or show how I feel
Because if I actually showed you
That would mean it is real

But right here, right now…it really does hurt
To pass you by and see you with her
For you, it might be just a game of pick and choose
And I realize I might be the one to lose

17. Fall

Those eyes sparkled at me
When I gifted a smile.
Embrace me with your odour
As I fall back onto the bolster.
Whilst you grasp me all over
I beseech for your adoration.
Bellow for your trace,avidly
As I think past those traces.
Hold me tight,fancy
Since you are a verve robber.

18. Stain

Showering with praises
There I stand as a newbie.
He took me along,tightly
The fear slowly crept in.
Shiver ran down my spine
I played along his tunes.
Tears fell apart from there
Color could only save me.

19. Home

A coffee shop in the midst August summer
Where it all began when eyes spoke
Followed each other's path in overlooking doubt
Hearts knew this was it, they are locked.
Pushed you into a puzzle
But you were ready to solve it to win
Could have ran away,but you stayed in
With a fire in heart and soul
You came to stay long enough.
Chaos flooded in from everywhere
But finally I knew I was home.

I Am Home

I had always written when I was at my most vulnerable either in love or heartbroken. The last poem which is called "Home" was written about the time I met my husband. I instantly felt I was home and that poem remains the closest to me.